Instinctual Poetry

Alden Landry

Presentation by *BookLeaf Publishing*

Web: www.bookleafpub.com

E-mail: info@bookleafpub.com

ISBN: 9789357612050

First edition 2022

I dedicate this book to my mom. I owe everything to her and her strength. Thank you mom, I love you.

ACKNOWLEDGEMENT

I would like to acknowledge my mom and give thanks for all her support and belief in me. I acknowledge that her passion for life set an example for me that gave way to me being a romantic dreamer, a poet.

PREFACE

Since I was a little boy I have loved writing and expressing myself. It is the best way I know how to express what I feel. I love well written poetry or lyrics from other writers. The sheer emotion captured in the message or the elusive wonder of what the message is; I love the infinite interpretations and bridged gaps in the void of human connection.

The right words strung the right way can shift the entirety of reality for an individual or even a large population of people. Words are magic. The words we speak are sacred and spells are being cast as we utter each heart felt tone through the soft lips of human expression.

Speak mindfully with the grace of your heart guiding the message you share. Honour, love, and appreciate this gift of life, as you spread the song of your soul upon this physical realm, with the words you do speak. Thank you.

Priceless Adventure

We drown ourselves.
In the chores of the day.
Tend to our routines.
We've been taught this way.
A new sensation.
A sense of thrill.
Can't be bothered.
We've lost our will.
Our problems do blind us.
Forgotten is the world.
Me, myself and I.
Are our favorite words.
Forever it may be.
But things can change.
And the people we know.
Are not so strange.
But people pass on.
We don't ask why?
Like the unheard song.
No effect, none to cry.
Sure it would be great.
And I can not deny.
That everyone would love.
The ability to fly.
So a journey worth taking.
Is what we need.

Though the priceless adventure.
Is life indeed.

-Instincts-
"it's not about what you know. It's about what
you feel. Listen to your Instincts!"

Dreams

Dreams are earned not given.
You may be stuck but you ain't in prison.
So get up out of your own way.
It's time to build, it's time to slay.
Build them dreams and slay them doubts.
In your heart you know what I'm talking about.
You got this, it's all in your hands.
You are magical, with a magic plan.
What plan is this? I don't seem to see?
Well, look harder, you can't ask me!
Look in the mirror and be real with yourself
Ask sincere and deal with the hell.
The hell you must walk through to find your true
voice.
If you can't see your dreams, you have no
choice.
You're likely numb hiding from your demons.
You ain't begun so you can't even see them.
They choke your soul and dull your day.
But if faced they too can be made to pay.
Tax them with force and face them head on.
Feel their presence and they will be gone.
Or continue to hide and they will continue to
haunt.
Blinding you from all you do want.

So if you're alive, I feel you're here for great
reasons.
Embrace your dreams and everyone of your
seasons.

-Instincts-
"it's not about what you know. It's about what
you feel. Listen to your Instincts!"

Win The War Of Life

Silence is so loud, when you want the answer.
Guidance is too proud, when you are the dancer.
Dancing all around, while the truth lies within.
Entranced with the sound of the avoided sin.
All the lies you tell yourself, to get through the
day.
Are big built up stories of what you'd rather say.
You'd rather be the hero and hold tight the glory.
But what if not yet is that your real story.
Could your story matter if it is not what you
want?
Or must you hide behind reasons of all you felt
did taunt?
Taunted by the sorrow of your forgotten pain.
You are echoed by the torture of the dragons
never slayne.
These dragons are yours and only yours alone.
You can face them or have a heart of stone.
If never faced, these dragons rule your soul.
Corrupting all your joy, they take a heavy toll.
But battles lost, do not declare the war.
They only define the moment and perhaps a
little more.
We define ourselves by the long road we endure.
Battles will be lost and so too our pride.

But we can win the war of life, if in ourselves
we confide.

-Instincts-
"it's not about what you know. It's about what
you feel. Listen to your Instincts!"

Parenthood

Fun times give way to much larger themes.
When you were getting it on, you may not have
seen.
Or perhaps you did if you were one to plan.
Maybe your little bundle of joy was a purposeful
command.
You knew so you went and away the shot was
sent.
Now I bet some days you sigh and repent.
Though not most I'm sure, you more often adore.
You are happy your child is here and for what is
in store.
But you know it won't be easy, and you'll have
to be less sleazy.
You're a parent now and it isn't always breezy.
You've got mouths to feed and forget what you
need.
Or at least get used to putting yourself last.
Your child will come first and for this, they
needn't ask.
You wanna see them grow and you wanna see
them shine.
Oh and you know you must invest the time to
nurture their mind.
Oh, it's all such a wondrous sight.
Watching them walk, teaching wrong from right.

Hearing them speak and laugh and even cry.
All of these emotions are such an epic ride.
So if your time comes, go on, embrace it and thrive.
Just know, please remember you are giving way to new life.
It ain't always rosy, maybe not intentionally chose-ee.
Done well though and you will take great pride.
Build a strong foundation and to you, they will confide.
Then this power of love will raise you high above.
Plus someday they can turn it back to you.
Once you wiped them, one day they will wipe you too.
The circle of life, and the circle of love.
When you are with your child you know they're sent from above.
A beam of pure light like the pure silk dove.

-Instincts-
"it's not about what you know. It's about what you feel. Listen to your Instincts!"

Silver Linings

If every day were great I think I'd smile a lot.
But days when it ain't I get shown what I've got.
A struggle in the moment can be hell beyond
relief.
Yet once it's come and gone, we see what life
did teach.
Yes, the dark does teach us how to feel the light.
Yes, the spark beneath us is ours only if we
fight.
Not amongst each other, but rather with
ourselves.
We have to dig deep, within we have to delve.
We don't always do this when left to our own.
So life provides pain, and once healed we have
grown.
People break our hearts and turn themselves
away.
Leaving us to ask "why must I feel this way"
We feel like running and we wanna hide.
This is when we summon all which dwells
inside.
We pull forth our strength and evolve to
overcome.
We stretch to great lengths and resolve all that's
come undone.
Resolve within ourselves and smile once again.

Solve rather than dwell, we let the joy back in.
So please if you are hurting right now.
Know in the future, you'll have done yourself
proud.
All of life is, from which you all can learn.
You just need your might, so as your view to
turn.
Shift and see what's shining, the aura around the
mess.
There is always a silver lining, and for this, we
have been blessed.

-Instincts-
"it's not about what you know. It's about what
you feel. Listen to your Instincts!"

Silence

What am I to write, well it seems I am not sure.
Can't find the light, no my mind is a bore.
Still, here I am laying down these words.
Fill this page again, maybe it's obscure.
Maybe my expression is not easily felt.
Maybe my confession is wanting to be dealt.
I do now confess that silence sometimes crowds me.
I may be a mess, I need the silence so loudly.
The silence speaks to me and shows me to myself.
This guidance frequently will save me from my hell.
The hell I visit exists only in my mind.
I needn't dwell there, nor drink the wine.
Rather I may ascend and feel my higher self.
The silence whispers "dear friend", break from your shell.
So while I knew not, what words I would write here.
Rather than be distraught, I let my silence steer.

-Instincts-
"it's not about what you know. It's about what you feel. Listen to your Instincts!"

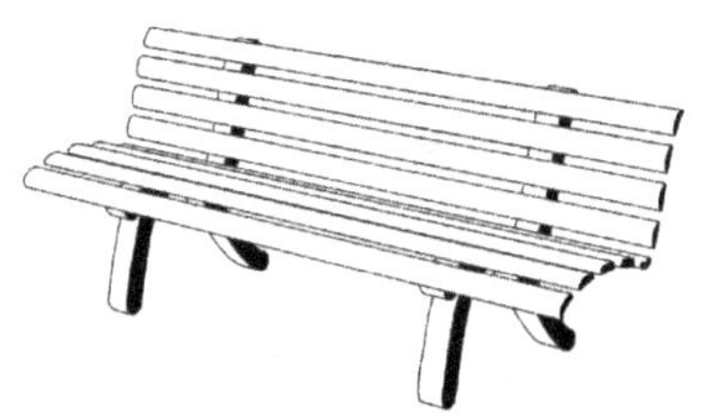

Untold

Squeeze my heart until it explodes undone.
Seize the start so it has not begun.
Hold back the fury of the angst in the air.
Dare me while I dare you, who really cares.
Maybe we both care, maybe we don't.
Maybe the chaos we can't live without.
Pouring my love into an ocean, so infinite.
Will the echoes of the splash return any minute.
Maybe I listen too hard to hear.
Maybe I should sing instead, it feels sincere.
The joy of my song is real, I know this for sure.
So lucky I am to feel this life I endure.
So now in this moment, while my heart quivers
in the cold.
I embrace my gratitude, knowing my story is
still untold.
Many chapters lie ahead, the journey will be
grand.
I walk through the shadows with ease, for I have
a master plan.

-Instincts-
"it's not about what you know. It's about what
you feel. Listen to your Instincts!"

Coffee

As the alarm clock starts buzzing.
You can't help but wish it wasn't.
Feet on the floor, yet you still don't adore.
If you're gonna give your all, you need
something more.
A little kick in your lazy little ass.
Luckily we got you, so hand over your glass.
Or your mug, you smug lil anti "am" thug.
A couple swigs and you're lifted by your drug.
Ready to soar and run out that door.
Take on the world this time for sure!
Coffee you see, she is the savior driving me.
Putting a pulse in my veins.
So I can grab them reins.
Today is my day with no refrain.
Medium, dark, light or decaf.
It's all gravy baby, so have a blast.
So smooth and tempting, it's pulling me in.
As I enjoy the full bodied bliss, I just gots to
grin.
Honey, cream, sugar or maybe just black.
Honey please deliver and I'll get off your back.
So if in the morning, you should rise before me.
You know what you got to do, put on that
coffee!

-Instincts-
"it's not about what you know. It's about what
you feel. Listen to your Instincts!"

The Touch Of Gold

Through trenches, you shall beseech.
Rusted wrenches twist to teach.
They twist your heart and your soul.
They twist apart your sense of control.
And while this torment takes its toll.
It is the storms of life that form us whole.
Without the dark what light would we see?
Without pain what would joy mean to thee?
Without loss would it mean to hold?
No, the cost must be paid, for the story to
unfold.
You must grind and fight, be daring and bold.
Then you may feel the touch of gold.

-Instincts-
"it's not about what you know. It's about what
you feel. Listen to your Instincts!"

Lucid Dreams

Off to a wonderland, I hope I can recall.
Oh yes, sandman, into you I must fall.
Falling and floating and drifting light away.
Involving all the notions of what I'm here to say.
Here I am now, to tell you to grab a hold.
Take back your dream state and dare to be bold.
When in a dream you can make it anything.
First though you see, you must possess the ring.
Become aware that you are not awake.
Then once aware you can really start to take.
Take off and fly, you can soar through the
clouds.
Make God sigh as he hears you so loud.
Oh yes, your heart will be alive and proud.
Be who you wanna, you can go anywhere.
Sleep with who you wanna, oh why would you
care.
You just wouldn't cause it's all make believe.
No need to give a fuck, so go and breed.
Or dance with the devil or the angels, either or.
Take a chance to hit the level, go on and max
your score.
Like a video game, you are the master, steering
reality.
Simply when you gather your mind, you build
all your steam.

Now with this steam, your dream is your machine.
Anyone can do this if they take the time to learn.
Through conscious intent, you can make this fire burn.
A dream is a dream but can also be much more.
Can be a lucid dream with anything in store.
With you as the captain, you can sail the high seas.
You can make this happen, with relative ease.
Through practice, concentration and desire in your heart.
Become a lucid dreamer, I know you will love this art.

-Instincts-
"it's not about what you know. It's about what you feel. Listen to your Instincts!"

You Love and Understand (to my Mom)

You brought me here with an open heart.
You sought my soul so (onto you) I would impart.
I've come to remind you of yourself.
In the dark times when you might forget.
I send you my love so you will not fret.
I shield you and protect you from harm.
Like you did for me when I was coming along.
You kept all the shadows at bay.
While you nurtured my heart so it knew how to play.
I owe all of the best of who I am.
To having had you for a mother and a friend.
You raised me to my greatest heights.
You loved me tenderly and you held me tight.
Then at times when I needed to learn.
You'd realign and become very stern.
Great strength was required to raise a son like me.
But you had what it took, for your heart was the key.
A heart so big, open and pure.
Like your loving smile, heart aches cure.
You always smiled when you looked my way.
Every time you did, it always made my day.

For you, I am grateful and blessed.
To you I must pay all of my chest.
My heart and my breath, both must honor you.
Along this paths test, I hope I am as strong as you.
I strive to meet the example you set.
To thrive since I'm alive, while my heart is kept.
Kept in rhythm to my own soul's beat.
Immersed in the prism of spirits, rainbow treats.
Yes you have showered me with the colors of life.
You love and understand and simply live life right.

-Instincts-
"it's not about what you know. It's about what you feel. Listen to your Instincts!"

You Belong

Beautiful people under the beautiful sky.
A serene unveil is this burgeoning life.
I love the moments, I love them all.
Even the pain, it shan't wear me dull.
Pain expands and pain does yield
A stronger you with which to deal.
So, embrace the strength life will give.
Feel the pain of the deep inserted shiv.
Life shivs us all in the front and the back.
Yes we are all under constant attack.
Unseen are the troubles as life unfolds.
Yet our chance may double if we can bear the
toll.
While eroding our edges the tide will do.
It can also carry to and from, the greatness in
you.
We are all amazing and struggle reminds us so.
So when it gets hard I wanna let you know.
You got this, you have been here before.
Not your favorite place, yet you've been able to
endure.
You made it this far and that wasn't easy but
you're strong.
Always remember you are a badass and this is
where you belong.

-Instincts-
"it's not about what you know. It's about what
you feel. Listen to your Instincts!"

Here To Help You Recall

Wish on an eyelash or wish on a star.
Dream all the while and wish from your heart.
Care for yourself and the life that you live.
Know that you will get as much as you give.
So give it your all, and always stay true.
Honor what will become the echo of you.
Find what you love and keep it alive.
Without passion how will you thrive?
Passion for what, you decide.
No one but you sees through your eyes.
Only you know what brings you joy.
Once you know, please don't avoid.
Keep that spark inside alive.
Speak from your heart and don't hide.
Be sincere in expression and teach the world a
lesson.
Set the example of being authentic.
Don't apologize, let them know you meant it.
We should all only be ourselves at all times.
We are all magical, we are all meant to shine.
So wish in your heart and dream with your all.
You are infinite, I'm here to help you recall.

-Instincts-
"it's not about what you know. It's about what
you feel. Listen to your Instincts!"

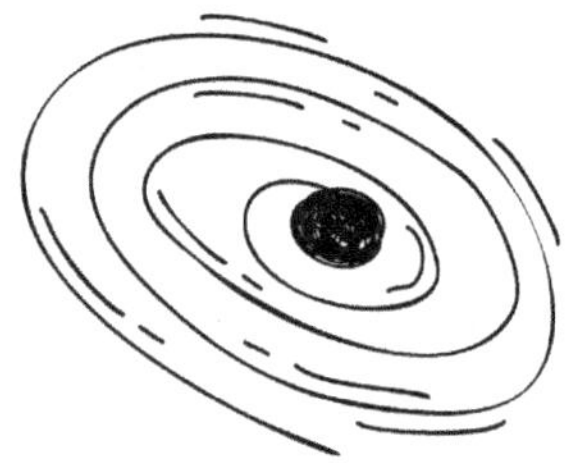

The Stars and the Moon

How to begin, surely with a grin.
Grinning as I express such a deeply seeded love.
A bewildering, passionate wonder, of all the
beauty above.
Sometimes I wish I needn't sleep at all.
With so much beauty, with which I can involve.
I love the sunshine, I love it oh so dear.
But I also desire to hold the moonlight oh so
near.
Sun gazing and star gazing I love them with all
of me.
Though because I am an artist, I feel more the
moon's gravity.
The moon is a receptive and expressive feminine
aura.
Hence why so many artists with the moon they
adore.
It amplifies expression and feeling into life.
It guides me away from the busy day's strife.
The stars too are special, each and every one.
They all speak to me and encourage me to
become.
The best version I can be, so as to shine just like
them.
Give my light to the world and the hearts which
need mend.

Thank you to the moon, and thank you to the stars.
Without all of your loom, I would surely fear the dark.
But the dark I never fear, no not even at all.
For I know you are near, and upon you, I can always call.

-Instincts-
"it's not about what you know. It's about what you feel. Listen to your Instincts!"

Crows

Eerie mysticism and magical ways.
Yes, the crow in my mind, how she plays.
She plays and casts her spell on my thoughts.
These days I ask her to tell me "what have you got?"
Is it one, two, three or four?
Unlike the Raven, it's not forever more.
Could be sorrow or joy.
Could be a girl or a boy.
Or maybe five, six or seven?
For silver or gold or a secret worth telling.
Or might it be eight, nine or 10?
A wish, a kiss or some joyous bliss my friend?
Whatever murder may appear.
I feel there is a message looming near.
Symbolic of mysteries and the power of insight.
Pay close attention when these birds take flight.
They may just reveal to you, secrets from which you rise high.
Like the wise crow, you may soar in the sky.

-Instincts-
"it's not about what you know. It's about what you feel. Listen to your Instincts!"

The Sight We Hold Within

Thank god, whoever that is, that I am alive.
God to me, dwells within, deep inside.
So thanks to me for making it this far.
So many times I wanted to join the stars.
Separate from this path and be free at last.
Yet I found my strength and continued on.
Knowing the pain was a sad guiding song.
Guiding me to where I belong.
The other side of who I am.
My full self, a true man.
With a heart of courage and kindness to share.
Without the sorrow, would I be prepared.
Not with the understanding I now have.
How we all suffer yet long to bath.
In the joy of life, we all wish to laugh.
When the bliss comes we know it won't last.
We long to hold it and make it all.
Forget the grief and hear only the call.
Of the joy we desire in our heart of hearts.
We want this fire to never impart.
Unite us with passion, with the breath of life.
Instill us with the ecstasy that is our sight.
If you see with your eyes you are blessed and
know this please.
Yet it is your mind's eye which sees your
destiny.

We all have access to the sight we hold within.
To see this is a gift which will free you from
your sin.
So please learn to practice and let the light back
in.

-Instincts-
"it's not about what you know. It's about what
you feel. Listen to your Instincts!"

Spill My Soul

Spill my soul upon this page.
Until this toll and gentle rage.
Pass me by and leave only bliss.
Try I must, whether hit or miss.
I'm here now, to let you know.
Given time, we all reap what we sow.
So search your heart for your true desire.
Perch and guard your authentic fire.
Let no one near that might lead you astray.
To reach the stars, your dues you must pay.
Yes, never stray from your real path.
Know it's for you, and that it will last.
Be true to yourself, first and foremost.
Free who you have shelved, let your soul be the
host.

-Instincts-
"it's not about what you know. It's about what
you feel. Listen to your Instincts!"

420 Ghost

Four twenty post.
I feel the 420 ghost.
She's calling to me.
"Set your mind free!"
Hearing her call.
I sharpened what was dull.
My senses heighten as I begin.
Forgetting all my sins.
Instead, getting lost within.
The love residing in my spirit.
With her influence, I can now hear it.
Lifted now as I write these words.
Not caring who might think it's absurd.
The herb and I, is mine to decide.
To cure the lie, I'm not going to hide.
Out in the open.
My heart's words are spoken.
Four twenty, I got mad love for you.
You connect me with all that is true!

-Instincts-
"it's not about what you know. It's about what
you feel. Listen to your Instincts!"

Not Such A Feat

Dropping mad words, cause that's what I got.
You may not have heard, I'm a lyrical nut.
I'm just the remedy, to all that hinders thee.
Bringing melodies', sweet and gentle therapy.....
.....Entrenched in an illusion, desperate for
repair.
There is no solution, my heart fails to dare.
Embraced by the music, it's soft and subtle
chant.
I dare to refuse it, and be all I'd thought "I can't".
I hold on to my strength, as my doubts melt
away.
I mold my sorrows into dreams, for which I have
paid.
Now the sun has risen, to light my way across.
Across the river, and through the valleys moss.
Once through the valley, the wind is soft and
sweet.
Come now shall we, it is not such a feat.

-Instincts-
"it's not about what you know. It's about what
you feel. Listen to your Instincts!"

Wake Up World

Walking through the valley, not a lot of connect.
Talking so proudly, yet they don't accept.
They don't accept because they just don't see.
They remain blinded by the hypocrisy.
It ain't their fault they've been led so far astray.
They've been culturally diverted by things so
mundane.
Phones, tablets, pcs and tvs.
The ego grows wider and it's me me me.
Plus no one has the energy to pursue their
dreams.
Or the courage or focus how could this be?
Exaggerating I am but I'm making a point.
It's only a few who don't absorb the anoint.
Who think freely, give it all and fight for their
heart.
While most others have theirs left in the dark.
It doesn't have to be this way if we can just
expand our minds.
See how their entire agenda is one big lie.
Stop being spoon fed your beliefs.
Believe in yourself and then you shall reap.
When you believe externally they take it away.
All of your power so they can enslave.
Your body, mind, and your soul.
All they truly desire is absolute control.

The power is ours, so let's take it back.
It's all inside once you get on track.
Learn to enjoy the quiet of your mind.
Deep inside we are all so kind.
So while they try to divide.
We must evade and unite.
Divide and conquer is fading away.
Cooperation will bring our glory day.
We don't need to compete.
Rather we must open and seek.
Seek peace and love and harmony.
Same as you want for your family.
Well, I'm here to state we're all a family of one.
Brothers and sisters under the exact same sun.
I love you all even when we fight.
We all long to set things right.
So Wake Up World.
Or we will never make this hurdle.

-Instincts-
"it's not about what you know. It's about what
you feel. Listen to your Instincts!"

Thank You

With vast dreams flashing before my mind.
My heart is dashing and so is my passing time.
Time stops not for anyone.
With every day, comes a freshly risen sun.
Upon the day I must feel my gratitude.
Yes, this way will heal my attitude.
With a positive approach, I move steadily
toward where I belong.
With each step closer, a little louder grows my
song.
Embracing the dance, I feel true that this cannot
be wrong.
Dancing to the beat of the drum within my heart.
Every chance I take, I stake on my art.
I don't mind the risk of running toward my
dream.
I'd rather shoot and miss than wonder what
could have been.
So here I am again, laying down my words.
Sharpening my pen, breaking from the herd.
Running free and true, expressing without
refrain.
So too can you, if you just give to gain.
See,my dream is to do what I love.
Have a real impact, and inspire the world to rise
above.

Poetry and music are all I wanna do.
So here I am today, practicing before you.
And if upon this day, you are reading these words of mine.
I now must stop and say, THANK YOU! For I need you to truly shine.
Yes without an audience, to appreciate what it is I do.
I would still do it for myself, but I'd rather include you too.
So know I am grateful, for all who read my words.
All who support my song, and all who encourage my birth.
The birth of my evolution is a forever flowing stream.
Yes, this surge of loving expansion is the stage beneath my scene.

-Instincts-
"it's not about what you know. It's about what you feel. Listen to your Instincts!"

Thank you

www.ingramcontent.com/pod-product-compliance
Lightning Source LLC
Chambersburg PA
CBHW072049150726
47996CB00015B/2424